T0158082

Life

How To Maintain your faith through adversity

Goes On

Allison Gregory Daniels

iUniverse, Inc.
Bloomington

Life Goes On
How To Maintain your faith through adversity

For information regarding permission, e-mail Allison Gregory Daniels at AllisonGDaniels@verizon.net.

iUniverse books may be ordered through booksellers or by contacting:

iUniverse
1663 Liberty Drive
Bloomington, IN 47403
www.iuniverse.com
1-800-Authors (1-800-288-4677)

ISBN: 978-1-4759-6719-7 (sc)
ISBN: 978-1-4759-6720-3 (e)
ISBN: 978-1-4759-6721-0 (hc)

Library of Congress Control Number: 2012923565

Printed in the United States of America

iUniverse rev. date: 1/9/2013

Contents

Acknowledgments

I extend my sincere gratitude to the following:

- The creator, through whom all blessings flow.
- My soul mate, Earl, for all of his love and support.
- My precious daughters, Kristian and Damona-I love you so much and I am very proud of you.
- My mom and dad who believed in me from the start.
- My sister and brother—keep on believing in God, and one day God will give you the desires of your heart.
- My family and friends for their support. There are too many of you to name, but you all know who you are, and I thank you again and again.

Introduction

Many blessings to you all! My heart is so excited about what God has in store for you and for me. To God I give all honor and praise for the words that He has placed into my hands to write this book. I pray that you will open up your heart and receive what God has to say especially to you. Whatever you're going through, you must trust Him and know that He is speaking directly to you in that area in which you need deliverance. There is a word in due season in this book for you because God's loving hand has directed my heart, mind, and spirit. I pray that this book will strengthen your heart so you can find a greater love from our heavenly Father as you move forward in your spiritual journey. I encourage you to read and meditate on God's Word daily to gain a closer walk with Him. A lot of time and energy have been put into this book because God wants you to know that *life goes on,* in season and out of a season. God wants you to know that even in your seasons of uncertainty, loss, and lack, *He* is still worthy to be praised. He wants me to let you know that *He* has you covered and that *life goes on.* So, stand up; rise to take your position as He is preparing to elevate you to your next level. Trust God to move you into your rightful position—because *life goes on.*

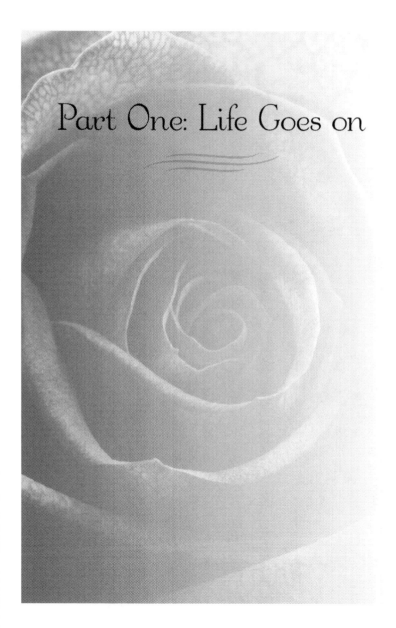

Part One: Life Goes on

Chapter 1: Life Goes on

Fear thou not; for I am with thee: be not dismayed; for I am thy God; I will strengthen thee: Yea, I will help thee.

(Is 41:10 KJV)

On January 3, 2003, I heard God speak to my spirit. He told me that I was going to go through some things in the next few years of my life that would shake the very foundation on which I stood. He told me that I was going to be attacked in several areas of my life, especially in the area of my faith. He said, *I have called you to come out from among them. You must be able to stand in order for me to take you to your next level. You must trust me like never before because I have placed a calling on your life and I have anointed you and appointed you for this season in your life.* He told me that this book was going to be the testament of my faith and trust in Him, for faith cometh by hearing and hearing cometh by the Word of God. As He continued to speak to me, He said, *You're going to face some heartache and pain, but life goes on. Know that you're going to face some disappointments and rejections, but life goes on. Yes, you're going to face loss and lack, but life goes on. So, "Fear thou not, for I am with thee: be not dismayed;*

for I am thy God: I will strengthen thee: Yea, I will help thee" (Is. 41:10 KJV).

I remembered saying to myself that God was preparing me for something I couldn't handle right then so I needed to continue to build up my spirit in order to face these future attacks. God's Word says, "Stand therefore, having your loins girt about with truth, and having on the breastplate of righteousness; And your feet shod with the preparation of the gospel of peace; Above all, taking the shield of faith, wherewith ye shall be able to quench all the fiery darts of the wicked. And take the helmet of salvation, and the sword of the Spirit, which is the word of God" (Eph. 6:14–17 King James Version, or KJV). I knew at that very moment that I needed to stop thinking about what I had lost in life and thank God for my next level. For the Word of God says, "Be transformed by the renewing of your mind" (Rom. 12:2 KJV). I had to change my way of thinking. I had to start speaking life to myself. I meditated on God's Word day in and day out. I thirsted and hungered for the Word of God to continually dwell inside me and strengthen me. I knew that I had to fall at His feet and lift up my hands and praise Him. The Bible says, "I will lift up my eyes to the hills—from whence cometh my help? My help comes from the Lord, who made heaven and earth" (Ps. 121:1–2 KJV). I knew that praising Him was going to be my way out and that I had to release those negative strongholds that had been placed over my life. I knew that God had placed something deep down inside of me, and I was ready to receive it. But, I heard God say to me, *Redirect your focus because life goes on. I'm getting ready to take you through some difficult experiences to strengthen your character, build your faith and your integrity, and to show you that I am able.* Early one morning, at around three thirty, as I was meditating on the Word of God, I had an out-of-body experience. My body changed from one place or state of being into another. I saw my spirit, all dressed in white, remove itself from my body, turn around, and look at me, and then it walked up a hill. My body was being transformed right before my very eyes. I was passing from one stage of my life into the next. But God needed to work some things out in me before He could position me. For the Word of God says, "To every thing there is a season, and a time to every purpose under the heaven. A time to be born, and a time to die; a time to plant, and a time to pluck up that which is planted; A time to kill, and a time to heal; a time to break down, and a time to build up" (Ecc. 3:1–3 KJV). I prayed that God would speak a word over my life and change it for its duration. I knew that the time had come for me to take my place in the Lord, that God had finally separated me from among my family, friends and co-workers. I had to answer the call that God had already placed on my life. Eternity had been placed in my heart to live out the will of and the call that God had over my life.

As I started walking into the calling that God had placed on me, I could hear God speaking to me about how to handle things and how to resist the cares and concerns of this world. Yet, some people started judging me. They wondered whether God had let me down or I had done something wrong. It seemed like the whole world had turned its back on me and walked away.

A friend of mine came to visit me, and I sat in my living room listening to her. She was like a sister to me and could see the tears flowing down my face. Without saying a word, she reached over me, grabbed my Bible, and started reading several Scriptures to me. Then, she said in her sweet, still voice, "It's going to be all right. You're going to be all right. God has you covered. God is watching over you, my sister, and God is going to bring you peace in the midst of your storms." And she sang a song with the line, "No weapon formed against me will prosper." Then, as she was leaving, she said, "Remember, 'The Lord is my shepherd I shall not want. He maketh me to lie down in green pastures: he leadeth me beside the still waters'"

(Ps. 23:1–2 KJV). When she left, I meditated on that Scripture over and over until it became a part of me and my transitional ministry. I started fixing my thoughts on Him and His power. It was very challenging for me because the devil had to now pull out his best efforts to try and trap me by setting a snare for my life. The word of God revealed that the devil was after my mind, my peace, and my life. The devil tried to destroy my life, but God was with me. My life was on its way to being turned upside down in a matter of months. "I have set the Lord always before me, because he is at my right hand, I shall not be shaken" (Ps. 16:8 KJV).

It was then time for me to stop pampering the things of the flesh and focus on feeding the fruits of the spirit of God. The Word of God says, "Behold now is the accepted time: behold, now is the day of salvation." (2 Cor. 6:2 KJV). I knew that God was going to finish what He had started in my life. So, I started getting up at five o'clock in the morning and meditating on His Word so that I could gain a closer walk with Him because the Word of God says, "My sheep hear my voice, and I know them, and they follow me: and I give unto them eternal life" (John 10:27-28 KJV).

I wanted to get in position to hear God's voice so that I could receive what God had for me. My transition period was a time of healing and a time for me to process what needed to be healed and restored back to life. God was getting ready to release His wisdom, His peace, and His understanding, as well

6

as His mercy and grace into my spirit. A spiritual awakening had finally been revealed to me. I had to get some tough skin in order to be ready for the attacks of the devil that were ahead of me. I needed to make sure that I knew that the value of my calling was not based on a mere man calling me. But, knowing that it was God who called me at His appointed time.

Life Goes On Prayer

(Psalms 26:1-7 KJV)
*Judge me, O Lord; for I have walked in mine integrity: I have
trusted also in the Lord; therefore I shall not slide.
Examine me, O Lord, and prove me; try my reins and my heart.
For thy loving kindness is before mine eyes: and I
have walked in thy truth. I have not sat with vain persons,
Neither will I go in with dissemblers.
I have hated the congregation of evil doers; and will not
sit with the wicked. I will wash mine hands in innocency:
so will I compass thine altar, O Lord:
That I may publish with the voice of thanksgiving, and tell
of all thy wondrous works*

Five Life Goes On Points

1. I challenge you to never give up.
2. I challenge you to never compromise.
3. I challenge you to never stop dreaming.
4. I challenge you to never stop trusting.
5. I challenge you to never give up hope.

Write down your thoughts, insights, prayers, or poems on the following lines.

_____

_____

_____

_____

_____

_____

_____

_____

Chapter 2:   Restoring Order

When a man's ways are pleasing to the Lord, He makes even His enemies live at peace with Him.

(Prov. 16:7 KJV)

During the most difficult times in my life, God asked me to uproot my life, leave everything that was familiar, and take my family into the land of the unknown. I doubted that it was God talking to me, but then I remembered the story of Abraham being told by God to sacrifice his only son, Isaac. Then I realized that it *was* God speaking to me. He was getting ready to restore order in my life. I came to believe that it was time for me to get closer to God. As a child of God, a daughter of God, I had to take my hands off of my situation and allow God to defend me. I knew that my heart needed to be in tune with God in order for me to hear His voice. I needed to be in a place where He could use me more effectively in a way that would show His divine workmanship. I asked God to humble me so that I could see His hand working in various areas in my life. I completely surrendered to my Lord and Savior to use me as a vessel for the ministry that He has placed inside of me.

One morning, I was awakened to God's gentle voice calling my name. I looked around to see if my husband had heard what I had heard, but he was sound asleep. Obviously, I was the only one who had heard Him. I realized that in order to follow God, I needed to get rid of the things that were not of Him.

Freely, I gave myself to the Lord and a mighty shift took place in my life. God was shifting things around in my mind; I wasn't thinking the same way anymore. He was also moving things around in my heart, preparing me for the ministry that He placed on my heart, which was to minister. God was ready to empower me to move to my next level.

Suddenly, I started remembering what my mother used to say to me when I was growing up. She would tell me, "Baby, you were born with a veil over your face," and I would say, "What does that mean?" She replied, "You can see things before they happen." As a child, hearing that truly frightened me.

I recall being a teenager in high school, when people often teased me because I was always on time for class, did all of my homework, and respected my teacher. Then, one night, God told me, "The one who keeps touching you on your shoulder is going to be involved in a car accident." When I went to class the next morning, this particular young lady wasn't sitting behind me, calling me, "Miss Goodie Two Shoes." Just then, the principal walked in and said, "Students, Toya was in a terrible car accident and didn't make it. Those of you who wish to have counseling, please follow me and a counselor will speak with you." I remember raising my eyes toward the ceiling and feeling very nervous and scared, thinking about what my mother had said to me. Later, God also showed me which one of my friends were behind my first apartment being broken into while I was on vacation. From time to time, He revealed to me if a person was for me or against me. And back in January 1993,

God revealed to me that my aunt was going to pass away one year from that day, and in fact, she did.

At this point, I asked God to stop revealing things to me because I wasn't wise enough to handle them. I didn't know how to disclose to people that I could see things before they happened. I was so afraid of the visions that were placed before me that I didn't recognize that it was a gift from God.

A few months ago, I was frustrated with a problem that concerned me. I cried out to God for answers because I was at a loss. My perspective on the problem became filled with stress, anxiety, and fear, but I wasn't going to change my position about my love and trust for God. In spite of everything that I was going through in my life, I trusted God. I still believed that God would be able to change my situation. Nothing that I was experiencing was impossible for God to change for His daughter Allison. The Word of God says, "Do not be afraid: do not be discouraged, for the Lord your God will be with you wherever you go" (Josh. 1:9 NIV). I prayed for God to bring comfort, peace, and quietness to my weary soul. I had to stop focusing on my situation and remember that goodness and mercy follows me all the days of my life.

Hebrews 10:22–23 (KJV) says, "Let us draw near with a true heart in full assurance of faith, having our hearts sprinkled from an evil conscience, and our bodies washed with pure water. Let us hold fast the profession of our faith without wavering; for he is faithful that promised." I knew God was changing things right before my eyes and that this old flesh wanted me to back down in fear. I understand that God's Word was placed in me to call on His name. "⁶ In my distress I called upon the Lord, and cried unto my God: he heard my voice out of his temple, and my cry came before him, even into his ears." (Ps. 18:6 KJV).

As I was being restored in my spirit, God was bringing me to a new level of peace and joy. I made up my mind that I was one of the ones who had made it through life's storms. Over and over again, I read the Word of God.

> Hear my cry, O God; attend unto my prayer.
> From the end of the earth will I cry unto thee, when my heart is
> overwhelmed: lead me to the rock that is higher than I.
> For thou hast been a shelter for me, and a strong tower from the enemy.
> I will abide in thy tabernacle for ever: I will trust in the covert of thy wings. Selah.
> For thou, O God, hast heard my vows: thou hast given me the heritage of those that fear thy name.
>
> Thou wilt prolong the king's life: and his years as many generations.
> He shall abide before God for ever: O prepare mercy and truth,
> which may preserve him.
> So will I sing praise unto thy name for ever, that I may daily perform my vows. (Ps. 61 KJV)

At one point in my life, my faith was under attack. Everything that I had learned in my life about God and His Word was under attack. I saw the motives of the people who called themselves my friends rise up against me. Eventually, I reached a point of brokenness; I felt as if I could not go on. Sometimes you come to the painful realization that you're just not strong enough to live out the call that God has on your life without giving your all and all to Him.

Even though we all face situations that seem impossible from time to time. I felt that my situation was unique. I had convinced myself that no one else has ever gone through this before and that I was all alone. I asked God why I was here, what was it that I didn't do or needed to learn in order to pass this test. I knew that I needed to redirect my focus. But, I wanted to give up and walk away from my daily disappointment because I felt that God wasn't listening to me anymore.

It seemed that I was in a valley of dry bones and God was far from me. Even though I couldn't see any light at the end of the tunnel. I still believed that God had my best interest at heart. I just didn't know when He was going to come through for me. But, I had made up my mind that I was going to trust in the Lord with all my heart and lean not on my own understanding. (Prov. 3:5 KJV).

Life Goes On Prayer

(Psalm 25 KJV)
Unto thee, O Lord, do I lift up my soul.
O my God, I trust in thee: let me not be ashamed, let not
mine enemies triumph over me.
Yea, let none that wait on thee be ashamed: let them be
ashamed which transgress without cause.
Shew me thy ways, O Lord; teach me thy paths.
Lead me in thy truth, and teach me:
for thou art the God of my
salvation; on thee do I wait all the day.
Remember, Oh thy tender mercies and thy
loving kindnesses;
for they have been ever of old.
Remember not the sins of my youth,
nor my transgressions: according
to thy mercy remember thou me for thy goodness' sake,
O Lord.

Five Life Goes On Points

1. Today, begin to restore what you lost.
2. Today, begin to rebuild what fell apart.
3. Today, regain your strength and begin again.
4. Today, remove the negative and press on.
5. Today, release the people or things that have been holding you back.

Write down your thoughts, insights, prayers, or poems on the following lines.

_____

_____

_____

_____

_____

_____

_____

_____

Chapter 3:   I Shall Live

He asked life of thee and thou gavest it him,
even length of days for ever and forever.

(Ps. 21:4 KJV)

One day I felt the pain of life pouring over my spirit. I had suffered at the hands of those about whom I had truly cared and loved. I felt that I didn't want to live anymore because so much was coming at me all at one time. It was in my moments of doubt that I felt God's hand on my situation. I remember constantly meditating on God's Word that says, "I have been crucified with Christ and I no longer live, but Christ lives in me. The life I now live in the body, I live by faith in the Son of God, who loved me and gave himself for me (Gal. 2:20 NIV). I had to stand on God's promises. I praised God for blessing me with a mother who praised God in and out of season. She kept speaking the Word of God over my life. She would say to me, "God has not given you the spirit of fear, so focus on things that He has done in your life this far."

Though I had already faced so many terrible situations and challenges, surely one more wouldn't destroy me. Even when I heard the Word of God speak to me through the pages of my Bible during my meditation hour, "Be still, and know that I am God: I will be exalted among the heathen, I will be exalted in the earth (Ps. 46:10 KJV). During one of the most trying seasons in my life, I knew that I was better off suffering a wrong because I was in my testing season and, this time, I knew it. I recognized it, felt it, lived it, and breathed it, and I wanted to pass this test so that God could take me to a new level in my ministry and trust me more. I wanted to go through this testing season leaning, trusting, and depending totally on God. I knew who I was in Christ, and I didn't have to defend myself before man. God's Word says, "Consider it pure joy, my brothers and sisters, whenever you face trials of many kinds, because you know that the testing of your faith develops perseverance. Let perseverance finish its work so that you may be mature and complete, not lacking anything" (James 1:2–4 NIV). I had to cast all my cares on the Lord and allow him to sustain me. I had to commit to the Lord if I wanted to grow in His Word.

Life Goes On Prayer

(Psalms 34 KJV)
I will bless the Lord at all times: his praise shall
continually be in my mouth.
My soul shall make her boast in the Lord: the humble shall
hear thereof, and be glad.
O magnify the Lord with me, and let us exalt
his name together.
I sought the Lord, and he heard me, and
delivered me from all my fears.
They looked unto him, and were lightened: and their faces
were not ashamed. This poor man cried, and the Lord heard
him,
and saved him out of all his troubles.
The angel of the Lord encampeth round about them that fear
him, and delivereth them.

Five Life Goes On Points

1. Learn how to live in the now.
2. Learn how to avoid negative thinking.
3. Learn how to handle a setback and rise again.
4. Rewrite some things you would change in your life.
5. Stop! Evaluate what you've been thinking about and change it.

Write down your thoughts, insights, prayers, or poems on the following lines.

_____

_____

_____

_____

_____

_____

_____

_____

Chapter 4:
The Purpose of My Trials

*My times are in thy hand: deliver me from the hand of
mine enemies, and from them that persecute me.*

(Ps. 31:15 NIV)

Each day marked the beginning of another chapter in my life.
The things that used to bother me, that used to make me upset,
and the things that had so much control over my life were now
being controlled by the Holy Spirit. I was being transformed
before God and man. People were asking me how I could
stand when I should be running and how I could smile when
I should be crying. God allowed me sufficient time to store up
enough of His Word in my heart, my mind, and my spirit in
preparation for such a time as this. His Word says, "Let us not
become weary in doing good, for at the proper time we will reap
a harvest if we do not give up" (Gal. 6:9 NIV).

I remember constantly saying to myself that I still had joy.
After all the things that I had been through in my life, I still
had joy. God was working things out in my favor. I know it
didn't seem that way to the world; I'm sure it looked like I was

going down, going under. I believed with all my heart that God was working things out for me, and I knew that I had the Holy Spirit living inside me. Despite what people said about my walk with the Lord, I was blessed because I was still alive. I asked God to "let the peace of Christ rule in [my] heart" (Col. 3:15 KJV). I remember lying across my bed reading. Psalm 27:

The Lord is my light and my salvation; whom shall I fear?
The Lord is my life; of whom shall I be afraid?
When the wicked, even mine enemies and my foes,
came upon me to eat up my flesh, they stumbled and fell.
Though an host should encamp against me, my heart shall
not fear: though war should
rise against me, in this will I be confident.
One thing have I desired of the Lord,
that will I seek after; that I
may dwell in the house of the Lord all the days of my life,
to behold the beauty of the Lord, and to enquire in
His temple. For in the time of trouble he shall hide me
in his pavilion: in the secret of his tabernacle shall he hide
me; he shall set me up upon a rock. And now shall mine head
be lifted up above mine enemies round about me: therefore
will I offer in his tabernacle sacrifices of joy; I will sing, yea, I
will sing praises unto the Lord. Hear, O Lord,
when I cry with my voice; have mercy also upon me,
and answer me

This Scripture didn't register with me until I was going through my trials. I had to tell myself time and time again that this was just a training ground for me. One thing I recalled was the importance of surrounding myself with people who love me and genuinely care about me. That way, when I went through my storms, they could pray for me. I walked into a room of darkness, and God became my light.

One day, I found myself sitting at a conference with my enemies staring me in the back. I didn't know what to say, so I just mind my own business until I was called to get up and speak. Several of those women went in and out of the conference room, trying to throw off my focus. In my earlier years, this strategy would have worked, but by this time, I was mindful of the enemy and his tactics. I had learned to turn my focus on God and allow Him to speak words through me as I speak life to His people. The Word of God says, "And my God will meet all my needs according to His glorious riches in Christ Jesus" (Phil. 4:19 NIV).

I had to continue to pray in the spirit on all occasions with all kinds of prayers and requests. With this in mind, be alert and always keep on praying for all the saints (Eph. 6:18). My spirit was being shaken because the enemy had peeked into my future. All I have left is a joyful noise to make unto the Lord for He has been so good to me. He has been better to me than I have been to myself. God preserved my life.

Life Goes On Prayer

(Psalm 31:1-7)

In thee, O Lord, do I put my trust; let me never be ashamed:
deliver me in thy righteousness. Bow down thine ear to me;
deliver me speedily: be thou my strong rock, for an house of
defense to save me. For thou art my rock and my fortress;
therefore for thy name's sake lead me, and guide me. Pull me
out of the net that they have laid privily for me: for thou art
my strength. Into thine hand I commit my spirit: thou hast
redeemed me, O Lord God of truth. I have hated them that
regard lying vanities: but I trust in the Lord. I will be glad
and rejoice in thy mercy: for thou hast considered my trouble;
thou hast known my soul in adversities

Five Life Goes On Points

1. Let your praise produce power.
2. Let your words produce your power.
3. Today, live beyond your feelings and your emotions.
4. You must believe that you are worth it.
5. Create your own affirmation and live by it.

Write down your thoughts, insights, prayers, or poems on the following lines.

_____

_____

_____

_____

_____

_____

_____

_____

Chapter 5:   Consider the Source

Greater is He that is in me, than he that is in the world

(1 John 4:4 KJV).

I can recall being very agitated and upset with a situation that had taken place in my life, and I totally lost all the peace and joy that was within me. Normally, I am a very happy and pleasant person to be around, but this particular situation took me off my focus and robbed me of my joy. I began to realize that I was no longer in control of things as I felt my emotional disposition change. There was only one way for me to find the peace and joy that was being drained from me; I knew I had to really seek guidance and instruction from God. He's the one who could restore things to order.

At times, you may not be aware of your surroundings, or even the person with whom you are interacting. You will find yourself entertaining another person's conversation, even if it is negative. For instance, I had a friend who—no matter what was going on in her life—was never satisfied or totally happy. She would constantly find ways to convince herself that others were being nice to her because they had been told to do so by their boss. She would begin making comments about me to deflect the attention away from her lack of confidence in who she was, giving me compliments about my hair and clothing.

Unfortunately for her, she was never quite the same after going through her second divorce. She started believing that, for her, true love was not obtainable. Because of her negative views of herself and other people, she faced various obstacles and pitfalls that became prevalent in her daily work, walk, talk, and life. She wanted to know what it means to be loved, how to laugh without covering up pain, and where to find that joy that could bring her solace.

My friend was not yet ready to release the negative mind-set that she had become so accustomed to for so long. Since I wasn't quite where I should have been to uplift her, I made the decision to separate myself from her so I could be rejuvenated.

Life Goes On Prayer

(Psalm 39:1-7 KJV)

I said, I will take heed to my ways, that I sin not with my tongue: I will keep my mouth with a bridle, while the wicked is before me. I was dumb with silence, I held my peace, even from good; and my sorrow was stirred. My heart was hot within me, while I was musing the fire burned: then spake I with my tongue, Lord, make me to
know mine end, and the measure of my days, what it is: that I may know how frail I am. Behold, thou hast made my days as an handbreadth; and mine age is as nothing before thee: verily every man at his best state is altogether vanity. Selah. Surely every man walketh in a vain shew: surely they are disquieted in vain: he heapeth up riches, and knoweth not who shall gather them. And now, Lord, what wait I for? my hope is in thee.

Five Life Goes On Points

1. Now is the time for you to reinvent your future.
2. Change how you view what you're going through in life.
3. Stop! playing the victim because you're a winner.
4. It's time for you to move forward in your life.
5. Choose the words you will use before you speak.

Write down your thoughts, insights, prayers, or poems on the following lines.

_____

_____

_____

_____

_____

_____

_____

_____

Part Two: Release Me

Chapter 6: Release Me

At the end of seven years thou shalt make a release.

(Deut. 15:1 KJV)

While driving with tears streaming down my face, I asked God to teach me how to remove these strongholds in my life. I said, "God, I know that you have given me the authority to discern strongholds in my life." As I reflected on the divine purpose for my life during my hardship, I realized that fear, worry, anxiety, and a desire to please people had a firm grip on me that needed to be loosened. I was ready to release the control back to the one who gave me life. I remember hearing God say to me, *You have too many people that have access to your life. Now is the time for you to separate yourself and release these people from you.* For the Word of God says,

"My thoughts are not your thoughts, neither are my ways your ways," declares the Lord. "As the heavens are higher than the earth, so are my ways higher than your ways and my thoughts than your thoughts. As the rain and the snow come down from heaven, and do not return to it without watering the earth and making it bud and flourish, so that it yields seed for the worse and the bread for the eaters, so is my word that goes out from my mouth: it will not return to me empty." (Is. 55:8 NIV)

My life seemed to take a detour. In (John 8:31–36 KJV), Jesus tells us that we can be held in bondage by strongholds in our lives, and His solution is to continue in His word. Verse 32 says, "Ye shall know the truth and the truth shall make you free" (KJV). My spiritual maturity came to me after I asked God to reveal to me the root of my problems in life so that I could stop blaming others and stop wrestling with the same old issues. I remember reading the Word of God when Jesus cast out a devil and healed a deaf and mute boy. Jesus explained that in order to overturn the works and activities of the devil, we must bind him first. "Or else how can one enter a strong man's house and plunder his goods, unless he first binds the strong man? And then he will plunder his house" (Matt. 12:29 KJV).

Releasing period 1:
Some people can't handle who you are, and some people are draining you.

Releasing period 2:
The day my dad passed away, I knew he was at a better home on high. But it took me some time to release him, and now I'm healed.

Releasing period 3:
Stop looking back for the things you've lost and the things man took from you.

God is getting ready to restore you like never before. At the end of seven years thou shalt make a release. (Deut. 15:1 KJV)

"For the weapons of our warfare are not carnal, but mighty through God to the pulling down of strong holds" (2 Cor. 10:4 KJV). Strongholds are torn down as we meditate on God's word. It's vital that you grow in God's Word because it is your weapon.

When you learn how to speak under the inspiration of the Holy Spirit, your words will take on a new form and give life and power as it enters into your heart and mind. Please know that you need God's power to be able to break free from the strongholds and that God's Word will reveal to you the areas of your life that have been controlled by your strongholds.

How To identify Strongholds

Point One: Identify the problem, the issue, and the source.

Point Two: Eliminate the problem and change your perception.

Point Three: Change your circle of friends and family and seek Godly wisdom.

Life Goes On Prayer

(Ps. 35:1-8 KJV)

Plead my cause, O LORD, with them that strive with me:
fight against them that fight against me. Take hold of shield
and buckler, and stand up for mine help. Draw out also the
spear, and stop the way against them that
persecute me: say unto my soul, I am thy salvation.
Let them be confounded and put to shame that seek
after my soul: let them be turned back and brought to
confusion that devise my hurt. Let them be as chaff before
the wind: and let the angel of the Lord chase them. Let
their way be dark and slippery: and let the angel of the Lord
persecute them. For without cause have they hid for me their
net in a pit, which without cause they have digged for my
soul. Let destruction come upon him at unawares;
and let his net that he hath hid catch himself:
into that very destruction let him fall.

Five Life Goes On Points

1. Today, ask God to show you the way, or your purpose in life.
2. Get out of negative thinking and live in the positive.
3. Start speaking peace over your situation
4. Write down your vision for your future and repeat it daily
5. Remember that Favor reigns over your life

Write down your thoughts, insights, prayers, or poems on the following lines

_____

_____

_____

_____

_____

_____

_____

_____

Chapter 7:   Revealing Time

Sometimes it was hard for me to look through my pain and see how God had His hands on me. I was going through so much disappointment, rejection, fear, hurt, and pain that it was difficult for me to believe that God still had me covered. But He has a divine plan for my life, and even though life throws curve balls, He is still in control of my destiny. God said, "I will never leave you nor forsake you" (Heb. 13:5 KJV). Many times God had revealed His plans and goals for my life in and out of season.

But I never expected to be sitting in a hospital room waiting for my four-year-old daughter to come out of emergency surgery. A few days earlier, we had to rush her to the hospital. I was sitting in class taking my final exam when my older daughter called me from home. It was out of the norm because she knew I was taking an exam and would not have disturbed me unless it was an emergency, so I stepped out of the room to take the call. She said that "Damona wasn't feeling well and kept complaining about her right leg hurting.

I said, "I will be home in an hour. Where is Daddy?" She said, "He's holding her right now." I said they should give her a nice, warm bath in mineral oil and massage her legs gently when she gets out, and I will call her doctor when I get there.

When I arrived home, Damona was sitting up but asleep. Around three o'clock in the morning, as she slept in my arms, she woke up in pain again. I placed an emergency call to her doctor, and she told me to take her directly to the children's hospital, nowhere but there because they specialize in children's care. I woke my husband and older daughter up and told them the plan—Kristian and I would take Baby Girl to the children's hospital in Washington, DC, and call him the minute we heard from the doctors.

Damona said, "Can we pray before Daddy leaves for work, and can you play my favorite song on the computer—'Grateful, Grateful, Grateful'?" We all tried to hold back the tears as we were getting dressed. We are a family that loves to dress alike, and we all put on our white Reebok shirts and red sweat pants. Dressing in our Reebok outfits brings us together as a family, as one.

We gathered in a circle as Precious Damona began to lift her voice in praise. "Father, please be with me and let the doctors help my leg feel better. Please give my mom, dad, and sister strength to hear the doctors, and hear our family prayers." After the morning prayer, my husband gave Precious Damona a kiss upon her forehead, and said, I"I love you, and Daddy will see you when he gets home."

Staring out the bedroom window, my daughter noticed her dad with his head down and his arms stretched across the dashboard of his black Mazda 626, praying. Well, about twenty minutes later, Kristian drove us to Children's hospital in her black Mazda Millennium. As we sat at the hospital waiting for Damona's name to be called, I told Kristian that the doctors would probably just give her some medicine and send her home.

Then, I could get dressed for work since it was only 6:26 am in the morning. Then, one of the doctors approached me and said, "Are you Damona's mother?"

I said yes, and the doctor told me that my daughter was getting ready to go into emergency surgery because of an infection. I hollered, "Oh, God! Hold it. I need to get three more opinions and find out more information." I called my husband and said, "You need to get here now. Damona is going to need surgery right now." Kristian and I called our pastors, family, and friends. I just kept praying, reading Psalm 91, and saying to myself, *God is mindful of you and your situation.* Well, when our family members arrived, several of them had on Reebok shirts and jeans. We gathered together in prayer. One of the nurses said, "Here is another Daniels family member. She is very well loved." When they rolled Damona away for surgery, she had fallen asleep, and all I saw in the room was tears in each person's eyes at seeing tubes all over her little body. Three hours went by, and we all laughed and talked about the goodness of the Lord and continued to pray. Soon, the doctor and her staff walked in with Damona wide awake. She explained everything to us, saying that Damona could either stay in the hospital for the next six months for evaluation or we could take her home and have a nurse come to our home twice a day to administer the medicines. We agreed that it would be better for me to take her home and that's what we did. After a week-and-a-half stay in the Children's Hospital, Damona and I were ready to go home. The nurse came into the room with our release papers and a wheelchair to take us to the front of the hospital. Seconds later, my husband pulled up in his black Mazda 626 car and lifted Damona into it.

Prayer changes things, and it changed our lives for the rest of our lives. We thank God for our pastors, family, and friends who interceded on our daughter's behalf for God to deliver Damona from what the devil meant for evil. God changed her situation and healed her from her head to her toes. Praise God forever more.

Life Goes On Prayer

(Psalm 91 KJV)

He that dwelleth in the secret place of the most High shall
abide under the shadow of the Almighty.
I will say of the Lord, He is my refuge and my fortress:
my God; in him will I trust. Surely he shall deliver thee from
the snare of the fowler, and from the noisome pestilence.
He shall cover thee with his feathers, and under his wings
shalt thou trust: his truth shall be thy shield and buckler.
Thou shalt not be afraid for the terror by night; nor for the
arrow that flieth by day; Nor for the pestilence that walketh
in darkness; nor for the destruction that
wasteth at noonday. A thousand shall fall at thy
side, and ten thousand at thy right hand; but it shall
not come nigh thee.

Five Life Goes On Points

1. Today, learn from your mistakes and make a difference.
2. Today, take responsibility for what you've done wrong and make a change.
3. Today, set healthy boundaries in your life.
4. Today, be optimistic about your future.
5. Today, smile often, laugh often, dream often, and love often.

Write down your thoughts, insights, prayers, or poems on the following lines.

_____

_____

_____

_____

_____

_____

_____

_____

Chapter 8:   Defining Moments

Stand fast therefore in the liberty wherewith Christ hath made us free, and be not entangled again with the yoke of bondage.

(Galatians 5:16 KJV)

Today, I realize that my defining moments are all related to the one main source in my life, God. I learned how to celebrate my life and my defining moments by taking my life one day at a time. I allow my heavenly Father to daily grant me His sufficient supply of love, peace, joy, strength, wisdom, and comfort that I need to make it through each day. Each moment in my life is a defining moment to me because I get to see the wonders of my God operating in my life.

Defining moment:
     When I am able to wake up and see another day, I know that God's been good to me.

Defining moment:
     When I am able to lift up my hands and give God praise, I know that God has found favor in me.

Defining moment:

When I am able to walk, talk, and clothe myself, I know that God cares about me.

So take some time out of your daily life and think about your defining moments that have led you to accept that God truly cares about you. "So, don't be not conformed to this world: but be ye transformed by the renewing of your mind, that ye may prove what is that good, and acceptable, and perfect, will of God." (Rom. 12:2 KJV).

Allow God in your **Defining Moment** to peel back some issues in your life that He needs to deal with, and He will perfect that which concerns you. Every morning, start waking up to the endless limits to what God has planned for you. Start building up your confidence in Him as dreams and visions are revealed to you.

Another **Defining Moment** came when I accepted that there is no true healing, no true deliverance, and no true recovery without God placing His hand on my situation. My father passing away was a **Defining Moment** for me. I questioned myself day after day about whether I had done everything that I could for him. Did I stay on the doctors and the nurses to make sure that they took good care of him? I learned so much in my pain and hurt that God revealed **Defining Moments** of strength and confidence so that I could endure through it all, even as I was questioning God, *Why? Why my dad?* But, I heard His voice saying to me, "Come to me, all you who are weary and burdened, and I will give you rest" (Matthew 11:28 NIV).

I fell into a state of depression and took on some symptoms of the flesh that were not of the Spirit of God. I began experiencing some symptoms of depression, such as feeling sad and hopeless and despairing. I lost interest in my daily activities like writing, exercising, and going to church. I lost my appetite and went through periods of not getting enough sleep, not being able to concentrate at work, feeling guilty, and feeling like giving up.

I had to allow myself to heal on the inside before I could be free on the outside. I had to forgive myself. I was totally broken, trying to reach a place of comfort. I had to change my way of thinking so that it could line up with the Word of God. I immediately started resting in the promises of God. I started making room for the Word to dwell in my heart and mind and began repeating Scriptures out loud to myself daily. Humble yourselves therefore under the mighty hand of God, that he may exalt you in due time: Casting all your care upon him; for he careth for you. (1 Pet. 5:6-7 NIV).

Life Goes On Prayer

(Ps. 65:1-4 KJV)

Praise waiteth for thee, O God, in Sion: and unto thee shall
the vow be performed. [2] O thou that hearest prayer, unto thee
shall all flesh come.
[3] Iniquities prevail against me: as for our transgressions, thou
shalt purge them away. [4] Blessed is the man whom thou
chose, and caused to approach unto thee, that he may dwell
in thy courts: we shall be satisfied
with the goodness of thy house, even of thy holy temple.

Five Life Goes On Points

1. What words will be your legacy?
2. Today, see beyond the hurt and live again.
3. Today, stay on track and let God be your guide.
4. How you respond to your hurts determines your next level in life.
5. Stop limiting God because your greatest joy lies in His presence with you.

Write down your thoughts, insights, prayers, or poems on the following lines.

_____

_____

_____

_____

_____

_____

_____

_____

Chapter 9:   Overcoming Hurt and Grief

God grant me the serenity to accept the things I cannot change;
courage to change the things I can; and
wisdom to know the difference.

(Serenity Prayer)

I can vividly recall the day when my husband and I went to our eight-month checkup for our little baby girl. Our nurse and several others came running into the room to put a heart monitor on me. I kept asking what was going on, but no one would tell me. They kept saying that the doctor would be there in a few minutes. The doctor asked my husband to have a seat and if our older daughter was with us, and she said to have her come into the room. The doctor held her head down, looked back up at us, and said, "I am so sorry. Your baby is stillborn. She didn't make it." I hollered out, "What? Why? What are you telling me? How could I go this long and not know that she wasn't moving, breathing, or kicking? And how could you not know?" She said, "Some people can go into denial, and that's what you did." The tears wouldn't stop flowing. I was so hurt, so lost, so angry with myself. My husband held his head down as tears ran down his face, and our daughter held her tears back as she was comforting her dad and me at the same time. She knew what we had been through to have this child.

This was the fourth miscarriage I'd had since we got married. My husband and I had been praying to have a child and were told that because I was thirty-nine years of age, we should try in vitro fertilization. Well, we did, and some days should have never been recorded in my life but I can't go back and change it. It will forever remain in the back of my mind. Did I do something wrong? I wondered. Did I move too fast? Too slow? What happened? It took a few days—not long—but I didn't want to come out of the hospital room. I closed the blinds and had the lights turned out. I asked my husband and daughter to leave me alone for a while and let me be to myself even though they didn't want to and the doctor didn't recommend it. She said that I would be all right because there was nothing in the room with which I could harm myself. "She just needs some time to accept it for herself," she said.

When we arrived home, we all went into our separate rooms and closed the doors in darkness. My husband came to check on me with tears in his eyes, saying, "Sweetie, just maybe it wasn't meant to be. Maybe God doesn't want us to have any more children." But I couldn't stop crying. I was too hurt to hear what he was saying because another life had just been taken from me, and I felt empty all over again. Our daughter came into the room, and we sat on the floor and cried together. Then the phone rang at about midnight; it was my doctor calling to see how I was doing, and I was still crying in the dark. I just couldn't believe that this was happening to us again. My husband had thought for sure that I could have another child because I had already had a daughter several years before we married. And this was his first child. Well, it didn't turn out that way for us, and we were totally heartbroken. After my family left the room, I told my doctor on the phone that I didn't want to live anymore, that I didn't want to breathe again, that I was tired, and that this was hard on my heart. My doctor said, "Allison, I too had a miscarriage before and was one day able to get through it and you will, too. You believe in a higher power, and He will see you through just trust Him."

Each day became easier for me, but I couldn't stop blaming myself. I asked God if I could be healed from this, and His answer was, Yes, you can. But there came a point in my life when I had to make a decision about whether I wanted to live or die. The Word of God says, "Death and life are in the power of the tongue" (Prov. 18:21 KJV). And I decided that I wanted to live and tell other people that they could make it, too. So, in my quiet moments, I had to meditate on the word of God. I created my own personal affirmation, and you can fill in the blanks.

Personal Affirmation

Today, I acknowledge that I've been hurt but I must go on.
Today, I will change the way I view things and how I view
      myself.
Today, I will learn to love again and laugh again.
Today, I _____
Today, I_____

   Each day, I would sit in my office with the Bible open, my
pen and my journal beside me, and jot down my daily thoughts.
In order for me to get through the healing process in my life I
started writing in my journal five things I wanted to accomplish
each day. Here is a sample of how I start writing in my journal
every day.

Prayers and Answers for My Daily Life
(Date) I want to inspire someone's life today (Date) done
(name)
(Date) You can put in your own daily prayers or requests.
(Date) I pray for deliverance in my life over _____
_____.
(Date) I'm thankful for_____.
   As I began to regain my confidence and my strength, I
started learning how to totally let go and let God. I started
seeing myself less as a victim and more as an overcame because
I kept on living even when the odds were stacked against me.
But I wanted to make sure that I understood what I was going
through. I asked myself two questions, and you may want to
ask them of yourself as well.

Questions and Answers

What is hurt? The dictionary says that it is the source of pain and gives trouble.

What is grief? The dictionary says that grief is sorrow, something that cause great unhappiness.

How to Handle Hurt and Grief

Start thinking about how this loss made you feel, and change the feeling into a healing process

Ask yourself what it is that you can learn from it and help others with.

Create a vision of yourself being at peace after the healing process.

Write out three of your strengths and meditate on them.

Write out three of your weaknesses and improve on them.

Schedule a set time to pray.

Schedule a set time just for you and God alone.

Ask God what areas in your life need to be lined up with Him in order to move on.

Ask yourself whether you are really a victim or a survivor.

Give yourself daily self-talks.

Healing Process Chart

My View	Things to Do	How to Release It
Denial	I had to acknowledge my loss in order to move on. Write your answer:	Pray without ceasing.
Blame	I had to stop blaming myself. Write your answer:	Ask God for clarity.
Hurt	I had to let go and let God. Write your answer:	Walk in love.
Darkness	I had to lift up my head and live again. Write your answer:	Write down your visions.
Doubt	I had to learn how to trust again. Write your answer:	Trust and believe.

As I started my healing process, I remember saying to myself that it's hard, but we all have to go through our own set of trials and tribulations in order to get us through our next levels in life. But I asked God after going through the loss of my fourth child what else could happen in my life. I had enough of the hurt, pain, and grief. Well, that is a question that I wish I'd never asked. I was not been prepared for the answer. As I fell asleep, the phone rang again, and this time it was my father's hospice nurse. She said that my dad had just passed away and that I needed to get over there as quickly as possible. I screamed at the top of my lungs, "Why? Why me again? What is going on? I can't handle another life being taken away from me. I'm just not that strong. God. Why? Why me again?" He said, *You're not that strong but I am and I will be with you.* My family and I hurried to my father's room, and I knelt down at his bedside to say good-bye. I said, "Daddy, I will see you soon. I love you so much, and I'm going to miss you." And

I fell into my husband's arms all over again, crying. You are never prepared for hurt regardless of how many times you've experienced it. I remember lying across my bed and looking out the window, asking God to give me His strength as I held the Bible close to my heart and began to read His words and cry at the same time.

Healing Scriptures to Use

- Wait on the LORD: be of good courage, and he shall strengthen thine heart: wait, I say, on the LORD. (Ps. 27:14 KJV)
- Let not your heart be troubled: ye believe in God, believe also in me. (John 14:1 KJV)
- And call upon me in the day of trouble: I will deliver thee, and thou shalt glorify me. (Ps. 50:15 KJV).
- Cast thy burden upon the LORD, and he shall sustain thee: he shall never suffer the righteous to be moved. (Ps. 55:22 KJV)
- "And we know that all things work together for good to them that love God, to them who are the called according to his purpose. (Rom. 8:28 KJV)

Chapter 10: Embracing Change and Personal Transition

EXCERPT FROM BOOK AS Co-Author-How To Survive When Your Ship is Sinking

A time to weep, and a time to laugh; a time to mourn, and a time to dance; a time to cast away stones, and a time to gather stones together; a time to embrace, and a time to refrain from embracing.

(Ecc. 3:4-5 KJV)

My Babies–A Lesson--Babies again! Falling in love was easy, and then came the question, "Can we have a child together?" Now that was something for me to embrace again because I had already had one child who was at the age of independence. Now that was something for me to think about! We needed diapers, a car seat, medicine, a doctor, some appointments, and so forth.

I decided to have my second child at the age of forty. With the first child I was a single mother at the age of twenty-five and felt too young to have a child. But, things were different back then. I had the patience to run from place to place when she had doctor's appointments. I had the time to spend on homework and school events. I had the strength to travel from place to place and not get so tired at one time.

With my second child was a challenge because my body was starting to change. My hormone level was fluctuating when I found out that I was pregnant and my husband and I hit some road blocks along the way when doctors were telling us that I was too old to have a child. I needed to take several test to make sure that my baby wasn't going to be deformed. But, we believed in God and knew that the Word of God said that He wouldn't send an imperfect gift. I knew in my heart and mind that my new baby girl was going to be okay no matter what the doctors had to say. I trusted the Word of God.

By my second baby's birth I felt that I was in between two worlds. I had one child that was getting ready to graduate from high school, and another child that I needed to nurture and embrace to that next level. I had to adjust my attitude and change my way of thinking because my patience had gone from me! Having another baby had no place in my life until I met the man that I married and loved him more than life itself. I wanted us to share in the joy of seeing our own child come to life, and God granted us that chance.

So, I had to learn to embrace the changes that I was getting ready to go through even with all of the challenges and uncertainties that were forthcoming. I believe that my transition to embrace this change made me stronger and wiser because I was able to grow and develop in the areas where I was weak. Patience was one of those areas.

Ten Points to Ponder

1. Step out of your comfort zone and live.
2. Live, love, and laugh more each day.
3. Enlarge your visions, your dreams, and your desires.
4. Change your perspective.
5. Create a balance in your life and live stress free.
6. Center yourself around positive people and people who care about you.
7. Be quick to adapt to new changes.
8. Speak positive words about yourself to yourself each day.
9. Break down the strongholds that are keeping you bound.
10. Let go of the negative, and let God's words heal you.

I believe that God will give us new strength. "For they that wait upon the LORD shall renew their strength; they shall mount up with wings as eagles; they shall run, and not be weary; and they shall walk, and not faint" (Is. 40:31 KJV). Each day, trust God to renew your heart and mind. The Bible says, "He changes times and seasons" (Dan. 2:21 KJV).

Transformation Scriptures

∾ Remember ye not the former things, neither consider the things of old. Behold, I will do a new thing; now it shall spring forth; shall ye not know it? I will even make a way in the wilderness, and rivers in the desert. (Is. 43:18–21 KJV)

- ❧ And be renewed in the spirit of your mind. (Eph. 4:23 KJV)
- ❧ "Wait on the LORD: be of good courage, and he shall strengthen thine heart: wait, I say, on the LORD" (Ps. 27:14 KJV).

Create Your Personal Affirmation

Today, I believe in change, and I believe that I will receive everything that I pray for each day.

Today, I plan to believe for the best in my life.

Today, I want to see change come into my new life.

Today, I give myself away to change by_____.

Today, I will commit to read a Bible verse every night.

Today, I will commit to pampering myself once a month.

Five Life Goes On Points

1. Today, Wait on God for your healing.
2. Today, live favor minded, and God will direct you.
3. Today, let go and let God change your situations.
4. Today, raise God beyond what you think your feel.
5. Take back your life and release the hurt.

Write down your thoughts, insights, prayers, or poems on the following lines

_____

_____

_____

_____

_____

_____

_____

_____

HEALING POEMS

I Want to Be Free

I want to be free from the cares of this world
I want to be free because I'm tired of the hurt
Each day I live I pray that You will
shelter me from the storms of life
And be with me now
My heart cries out and my feelings know of no other
Comforter but You
I want to be free from the cares of this world

WALK AHEAD OF ME, GOD

Help me to continue to trust in you
Help me to continue to believe that you will
see me through
Help me to commit this day to you
And help me to commit my family, too
Help me to stand in bad times and
Help me to stand in good times
Help me to be content in whatever state I'm in
Walk ahead of me God and pave my way
Speak your words through me today
Help me to hold my peace even in my storms
Help me to do my part and to move on
Help me to press on to higher heights
Help me to stay focused on your light
Help me to hold out, help me to stand

Help me to do the best that I can
Help me to expect the unexpected today
And help me to walk along in your way
ever state I am in
And help me to know that you are my friend

I'M TAKING BACK MY LIFE

I'm taking back my life
Though I can't change what has happened to me
I can make a difference in my future you see
Yes, I'm taking back my life because I have a choice
Can you hear the victory in my voice
Can you see the determination in my eyes
So, now I rise
I'm pressing on, I'm moving on, I'm continuing on
I'm learning how to move pass my storms
Because I'm determined to take back my life
Yes, I survived, I made it over, I've made
it through
I'm determined to do what I must do
Though I may have been battered, beaten and scared
Though I was a victim of an unjust cause

Though I wanted to run away just from it all
Today, I'm standing tall
I don't have my back up against the wall
See, the joy I used to have I'm taking it back
The peace I used to have I'm taking it back
The love I used to have I'm taking it back
And so now I challenge you today
To continue to believe in yourself
Today, I challenge you, dare to dream
Don't give up, don't give in, hold out and hold on

NOT WELCOMED

Have you ever felt not welcomed in a place?
Not because of the color of your skin
Not because of the clothes you wear
Not because of the company you keep
But because of the way you carry yourself

Even if you smile a lot, those who are miserable
Will find a way to crush your spirit
Even if you laugh too much, then those who are unhappy
Will try to find a way to make you cry
Even if you say a kind word or two, the jealous ones
Will somehow always find fault in you
Even if you are too quiet, those who are loud
Will find a way to stand out in the crowd

Have you ever felt not welcomed in a place?
Not because of the education that you have
Not because of how outspoken you are
Not because of the amount of money you have
But because of the way you carry yourself

NO MORE HURT

No more hurt
I'm placing it in the dirt
Verbal abuse
Child abuse
And domestic violence

No more hurt
I'm placing it in the dirt
Low self-esteem
Mere depression
Being afraid

FIND YOUR PLACE

Find your place in life
Find your dream and live it out
Don't be so easy to take in the doubt
Take a stand
You can make it
If you believe you can
Know who you are and where you're going
And how you're going to get there
For the future helps you deal with the past
That you can not change
Just believe that what you missed today
Will be gained tomorrow
Learn to let go and move on
For within you lies hope for tomorrow
Press on a few more seconds

A few more hours
A few more days
And let hope show you the way
Reach for that which seems out of reach
And have enough faith to move mountains
And have enough faith to hold on a little bit longer
And find your place in life

ME

You thought you had me bound
But I've placed my feet on holy ground
And now I'm coming around

You thought you took my joy away
But now I'm living another day
Just so that I can say
I'm still alive

You thought you stole my peace
But now my peace has increased
Because God has caused the hatred to cease

I WILL SURVIVE

I will survive without you
I'm living my life without you
I'm making a new change in myself
I'm speaking up and speaking out
I'm learning how to deal with the encounters
I had to face along the way
I will survive without you
I may be press down but I'm pressing up
I may stumble and fall
But I'm knocking down that wall
Because I want to live
I will survive without you
Because I'm determined to see my change come true
I've decided to resist the negative forces in my life
And rise to a higher level
I will survive

NO CHAINS

NO CHAINS
I felt your chains before
Trying to hold me down once more
But I'm sure
I'm stopping this cycle of events
Before you try to build a fence around my heart

NO CHAINS
I felt you try to detain me
By putting a strain, on me
As the shackles tried to restrain me
Quickly I detached myself
From the bond you held for me

NO CHAINS
I felt I was being confined
Like there were limits on lifeline
Pinching me in the spine
Choking me with time
Trying not to let me find
My peace of mind

NO CHAINS

I AM A ROSE

A rose means so much
When only one is given
Expressions from the mind, heart, body and soul
There's so much more to behold
In a single rose
I AM A ROSE
For there is so much more to me to see
As a rose
I'm special when held with two hands
Gently pressed against one's heart
Hoping that one understands the meaning of a single rose
Yes, a rose I call myself
Because I can capture the beauty of one's
own imagination enlightening the heart and
Uplifting the spirit
As a rose
I bring joy to life and laughter to your heart
I'm a vision of beauty a beacon of light
Adding much sunshine to your nights
I AM A ROSE

NOT ACCOUNTED

I am not accounted for your actions toward me
I am not accounted because I smile all the time
I am not accounted because of the color of my skin

BUT, STILL I GOT BLAMED

I am not accounted because I don't talk a lot
I am not accounted because you take my silence
as being mean
I am not accounted because your life is empty inside

BUT, STILL I GOT BLAMED

I am not accounted because you're lonely
I am not accounted because you're miserable
I am not accounted because you are unhappy at home

BUT, STILL I GOT BLAMED

I am not accounted because I don't talk a lot
I am not accounted because you take my silence
as being mean
I am not accounted because your life is empty inside

HELD FOR A 100 DAYS

I know what it feels like to be held for 100 days
To be held at a job, to be in captivity
No where to run, no where to go, no where to hide
To not be able to leave your job because you
are concerned about keeping a roof over your head,
food on the table and clothes on your back
I know what it feels like to be held for 100 days
To have someone tell you that you have to stay until
they find a replacement for you because without
you the job would fall apart
But, I remember being told by my supervisor that I did
nothing all day
I remember getting an unsatisfactory rating on
my evaluation

I remember being harassed, questioned and accused by
My supervisor when things went wrong
So, I know what it feels like to be held for 100 days
Trying to hold back the tears, the sorrow, the bitterness
Trying not to give up nor give in
Trying to keep your cool though you know that this is
another way for them to try and bring you down
I know what it feels like to be held for 100 days

WHERE

Where there is love, there is sorrow
Time just keeps pressing on
Where there is happiness, there is sadness
Time just keeps pressing on
Where there is joy, there is pain
Time just keeps pressing on
Where there is peace, there is conflict
Time just keeps pressing on
Where there is calmness, there is confusion
Time just keeps pressing on
Where there is pleasure, there is strife
Time just keeps pressing on

FALLING VICTIM

Falling victim, I felt I was
Trying to keep peace on my job
I only hurt myself
I was the laughing stock
I was the one that people preyed on
I was the center of their stupidity

Falling victim, I felt I was
Trying to keep peace on my job
I was the one marked as an angry employee
I was the target of their attention
For some I was their scape goat
But, for others, it was just a game

I FOUND LOVE

I found love within myself
I found my love like nothing else
I have peace within myself
That I didn't know I had
But I'm surely glad
That the joy of knowing fell on me
When I opened my eyes to see
I have happiness as deep as the sea
For I found love inside of me

YOU ARE MY STRENGTH

Here I am walking with no one else
Traveling a path with just myself
I'd given up waiting for others to help
And trusting in promises that are not kept
I've tried many things, I've gone to great lengths
To find after all that you are my strength
Like a bright light you've always shined
Lightning the way so that I might find
Tranquility and calm and peace in my mind
Leaving the darkness and troubles behind
From the twelfth of never to forever the tenth
I couldn't have made it without you
You are my strength

THINK ABOUT ME

Close your eyes and think about me
And I will be whatever you can see
Hold my hand and touch my heart
Because I believe that we will never part
Call my name no matter where you are
For I am at a distance not that far
You can reach for me at any time
For I am now a part of your mind
I will always love and cherish you
I will always be there to see you through
My love for you is as deep as the ocean
Tapping the core of all of my emotions
Close your eyes and think about me

WITHIN YOU

I can feel the hurt within you
I can see exactly what you're going through
I have no words to ease your pain
I don't know how it all began
But I am here for you and I understand
For I can feel the hurt within you

I will be there beside you when you cry
I will carry and comfort you by and by
And when your dreams abruptly end
You can count on me, I am your friend
Because I am confident within my mind
I'll be there for you til the end of time
I can feel the hurt within you

Prayer of Salvation

If you would like to receive all that Jesus has done for you and make Him your Lord and Savior, please pray this prayer:

Dear heavenly Father, I come to You right now asking for Your forgiveness. I am a sinner, and I want to repent. I make the decision right now of my own will to turn away from my sins and turn to You. Your Word says that if I confess with my mouth and believe in my heart that Your Son, Jesus, died for my sins and rose from the dead, I shall be saved (Rom. 10:9). I confess this now and do believe it in my heart. I submit my life to You. Thank You for saving me and giving me Your Holy Spirit, who will now live in me and help me to obey You and live by Your Word. Thank you for giving me eternal life, and filling my heart with your peace and joy. Amen

About the Author

Allison Gregory Daniels is president and CEO of ADG Enterprises and All God's Doing Ministries. She conducts workshops and seminars that are presented throughout the United States and abroad. These workshops and seminars focus on topics such as women in management, women as leaders, the Superwoman syndrome, leadership skills, the assertive woman, and diversity and emotional wellness for women. Daniels has been certified by the Professional Women Network as a Professional Coach and Diversity Consultant.

Allison Gregory Daniels has been performing in the arenas of television, radio, and stage for several years. She held her first poetry and inspirational book signing at Adelia's Restaurant in Takoma Park, Maryland, in 1999. Over the years, she has authored over one thousand poems and had several published.

She has also donated several of her poems to the local newspapers throughout the Washington, DC, metropolitan area.

If you would like to contact Allison Gregory Daniels, you may do so at any of the following:

P. O. Box 1571
Clinton, MD 20735
(202) 258-4987
www.AllisonGDaniels.com
www.allgodsdoingministries.com
E-mail: AllisonGDaniels@verizon.net

For more information about hiring Allison Gregory Daniels for poetry readings, book signings, workshops, organization events, private parties, business and corporate functions, public speaking for schools, church or other community events, contact her online at AllisonGDaniels@verizon.net.

Other Books by the Author

Black Man I Love You
Comfort Corner
Daily Words of Wisdom
Facing Tomorrow
A Glimpse of Glory
I Dream in Colors
Jesus, a Joy to Call My Own
Love Expressed through a Poet
Mother, I Love You
Poems for All Occasions
Revitalizing Your Spirit
Spirit of a Woman: Tribute to Oprah Winfrey
Sweet Memories of Yesterday
Taking Back My Life
Tribute to President Obama
Yearning for Love (first published book)

Books Coauthored by Allison Gregory Daniels

Celebration of Life: Inspirations for Women
How to Survive When Your Ship Is Sinking (Weathering Life's Storms)
Releasing Strongholds (Letting Go of what's holding you back)